# HOW TO TELL

# IF YOU ARE HUMAN

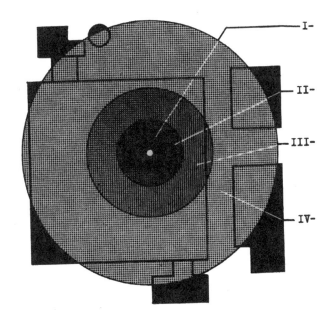

# HOW TO TELL

# IF YOU ARE HUMAN

DIAGRAM POEMS BY

# JESSY RANDALL

PLEIADES PRESS

ISBN: 978-0-8071-6984-1

Published by Pleiades Press

Department of English
University of Central Missouri
Warrensbsurg, Missouri 64093

Distributed by Louisiana State University Press

Design and layout by David Wojciechowski / www.davidwojo.com

Author photo by Byran Oller

First Pleiades Printing, 2018

The author gratefully acknowledges the editors of the literary journals and anthologies in which these diagram poems first appeared, sometimes in slightly different form:

*A Bad Penny Review, Bateau, The Best American Experimental Writing 2015, concis, Eunoia, Jubilat, Juked, M58, Mama Liberada, Maudlin House, Menacing Hedge, Ohio Edit, petrichor, Pilgrimage, Pleiades, Poetry, Poetry Northwest, Rattle, Really System, Scud, Section 8, Timber Journal,* and *Vector.*

Financial Assistance for this project has been provided by the Missouri Arts Council, a state agency, and the National Endowment for the Arts.

*for Ross, Will, and Celie*

# CONTENTS

PART 3: BE YOURSELF (BUT NOT TOO MUCH)

# PART 1

# THEY FINALLY FIGURED OUT
# WHAT'S WRONG WITH YOU

Do you ever sing a song to yourself in your car and you stop at a red light and your windows are down and you glance over and the person next to you has her window down and you wonder if she's listening to the same station on the radio and if she is, is she singing along and are you doing a duet? Will she smile at you and think this is amazing, or will she ignore you because she thinks she's a better singer? Maybe she's in a band and she's going to pull over at the side of the road up ahead and next thing you know you're singing back-up in a band with her wearing similar-but-not-identical black dresses and which of you will get the sexier one? And then you'll have an argument and the band will break up all because of your vanity.

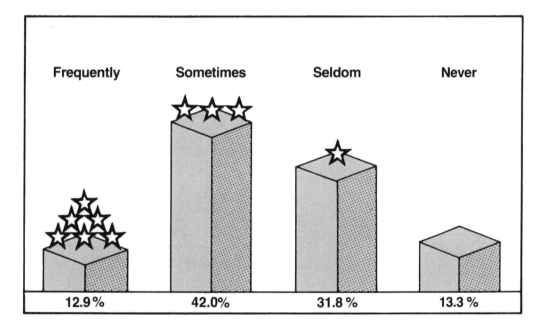

| Frequently | Sometimes | Seldom | Never |
|:---:|:---:|:---:|:---:|
| 12.9% | 42.0% | 31.8% | 13.3% |

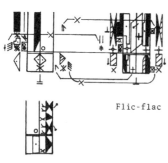 sorry mom I didn't hear you

Flic-flac

 I heard you
I'll be right down

 just let me die
one more time

 mom, seriously,
I only just got on

 I can't stop now
it's an important part

 aw mom
five more minutes

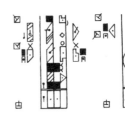

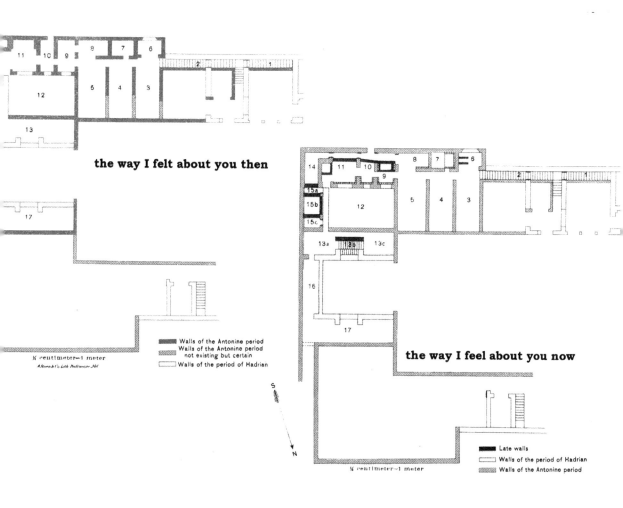

the way I felt about you then

Walls of the Antonine period
Walls of the Antonine period
not existing but certain
Walls of the period of Hadrian

½ centimeter=1 meter
A Hoen & Co Lith Baltimore Md

the way I feel about you now

Late walls
Walls of the period of Hadrian
Walls of the Antonine period

½ centimeter=1 meter

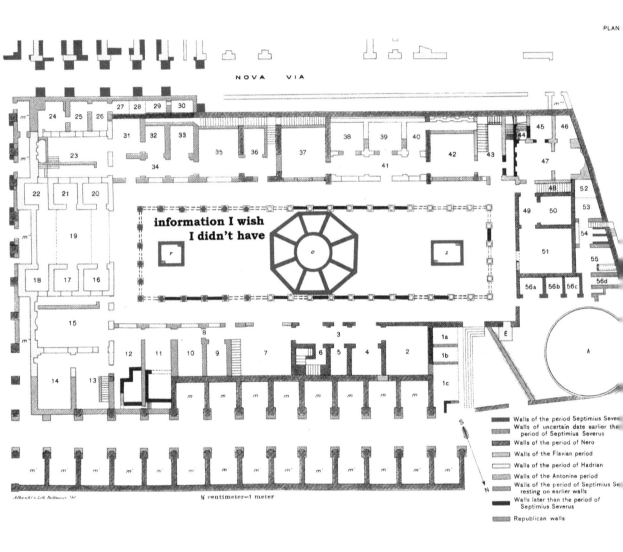

PLAN

NOVA VIA

27 28 29 30

24 25 26

m⁻

31 32 33

23

35 36 37

34

38 39 40

42 43

41

44 45 46

47

22 21 20

m⁻

19

information I wish
I didn't have

r

o

s

48 52

49 50 53

54

51

55

18 17 16

15

56a 56b 56c

56d

8

3

12 11 10 9 7

6 5 4 2

1a

1b

14 13

m m m m m m m m

1c

E

A

S

N

½ centimeter=1 meter

Walls of the period Septimius Sever
Walls of uncertain date earlier the
period of Septimius Severus
Walls of the period of Nero
Walls of the Flavian period
Walls of the period of Hadrian
Walls of the Antonine period
Walls of the period of Septimius S
resting on earlier walls
Walls later than the period of
Septimius Severus
Republican walls

PLAN D

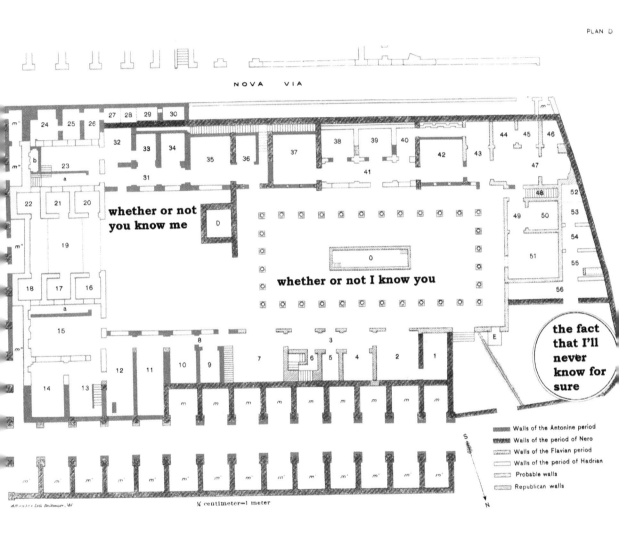

NOVA VIA

whether or not
you know me

whether or not I know you

the fact
that I'll
never
know for
sure

Walls of the Antonine period
Walls of the period of Nero
Walls of the Flavian period
Walls of the period of Hadrian
Probable walls
Republican walls

¼ centimeter=1 meter

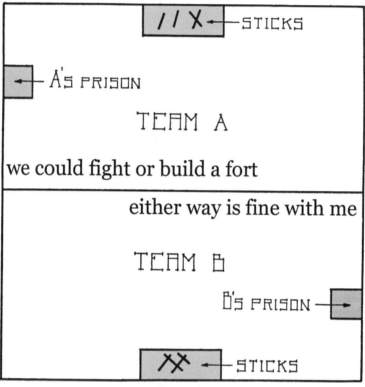

FIGURE 38.

# IS IT A BOY OR A GIRL

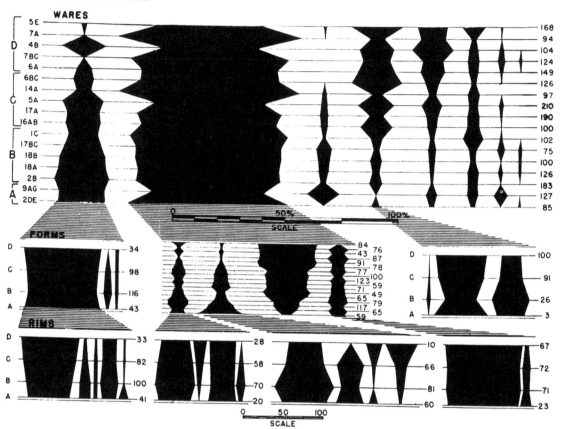

## WHAT COLOR SHOULD WE PAINT THE WALLS

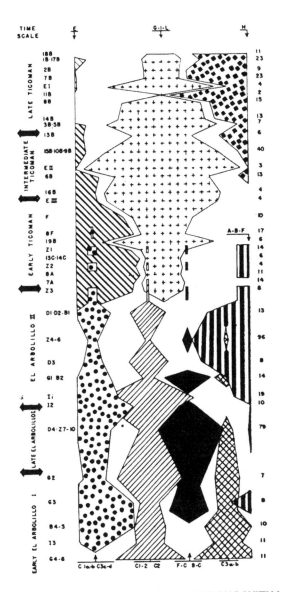

**THEY FINALLY FIGURED OUT WHAT'S WRONG WITH YOU**

I didn't ask for your advice

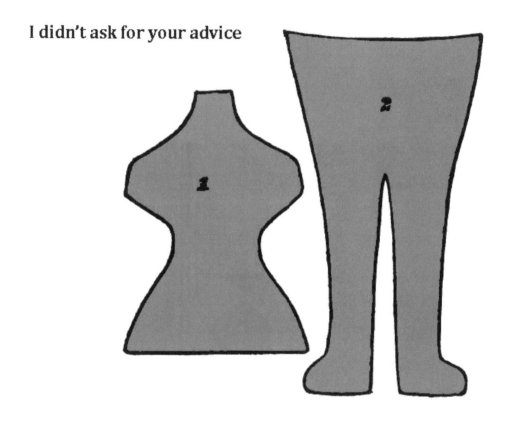

46. Sing a song or take a hint.

47. Perform the laughing gamut, without a pause or mistake : —

                    ha !
            ha !        ha !
        ha !                ha !
      ha !                    ha !
       ha !                    ha !
     ha !                        ha !
    ha !                          ha !
  ha !                              ha !

48. **Keep silence and** don't talk about anything that matters to you. If you accidentally say something real, cover it up with no. 47. Go home early and wonder what you missed. Probably nothing.

49. **Kiss your shadow in every corner of the room without langhing.**

# CLICK ON THE IMAGE
# NOTHING WILL HAPPEN

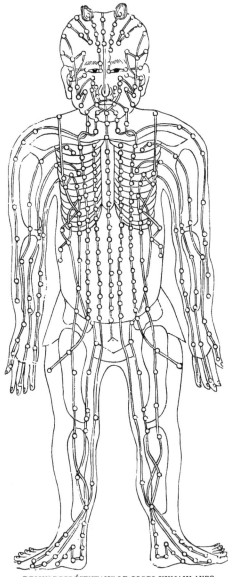

DESSIN REPRÉSENTANT LE CORPS HUMAIN AVEC
LES ENDROITS OU L'ON PEUT PIQUER.

# CLICK OVER AND OVER
# NOTHING WILL CHANGE

PLANT BACTERIA-VOL 3.                                    PLATE 44.

**1st period 8:01-8:56**

you have English I have social studies

**2nd period 8:59-9:54**

you have PE I have math

**3rd period 9:57-10:52**

you have social studies I have PE

**4th period 10:55-11:50**

we both have Spanish

you sit 2 desks back and 1 over

1

2

3

4

**5th period 11:53-12:13 LUNCH**

you sit with Jeremy and those guys at corner table

**6th period 12:16-1:11**

you have math I have English

**7th period 1:14-2:09**

we both have biology

we are lab partners! Don't talk so much. Let HIM talk.

**8th period 2:12-3:07**

you have band I have choir

after school you have soccer I have play rehearsal

if I go home the long way I can see you from very far off

5

6

7

8

57

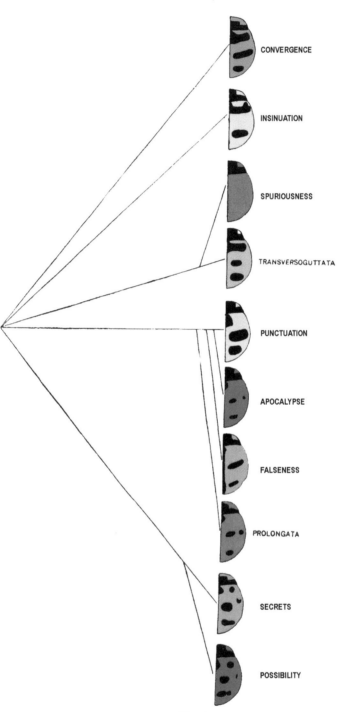

CONVERGENCE

INSINUATION

SPURIOUSNESS

TRANSVERSOGUTTATA

PUNCTUATION

APOCALYPSE

FALSENESS

PROLONGATA

SECRETS

POSSIBILITY

FIG. 47.

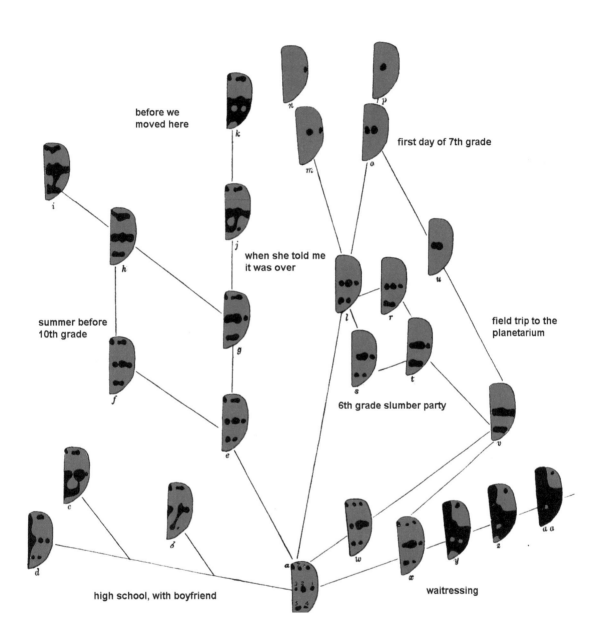

before we
moved here

first day of 7th grade

when she told me
it was over

summer before
10th grade

field trip to the
planetarium

6th grade slumber party

high school, with boyfriend

waitressing

PLATE 14

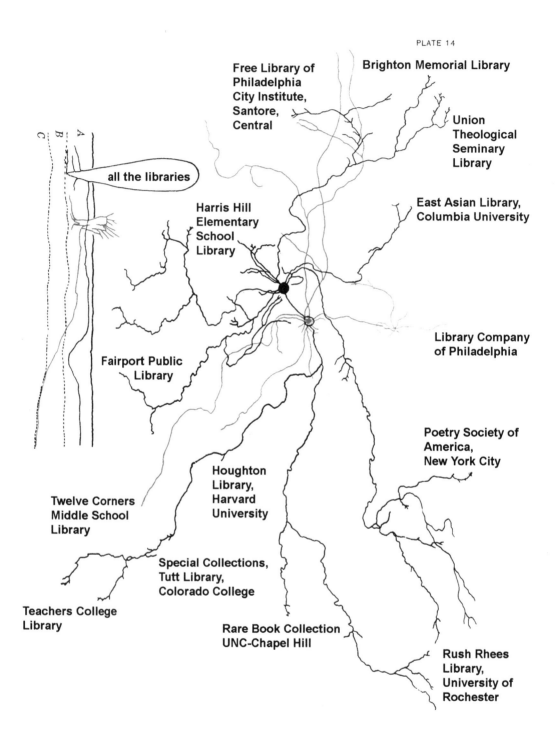

Free Library of Philadelphia City Institute, Santore, Central

Brighton Memorial Library

Union Theological Seminary Library

all the libraries

Harris Hill Elementary School Library

East Asian Library, Columbia University

Fairport Public Library

Library Company of Philadelphia

Poetry Society of America, New York City

Twelve Corners Middle School Library

Houghton Library, Harvard University

Teachers College Library

Special Collections, Tutt Library, Colorado College

Rare Book Collection UNC-Chapel Hill

Rush Rhees Library, University of Rochester

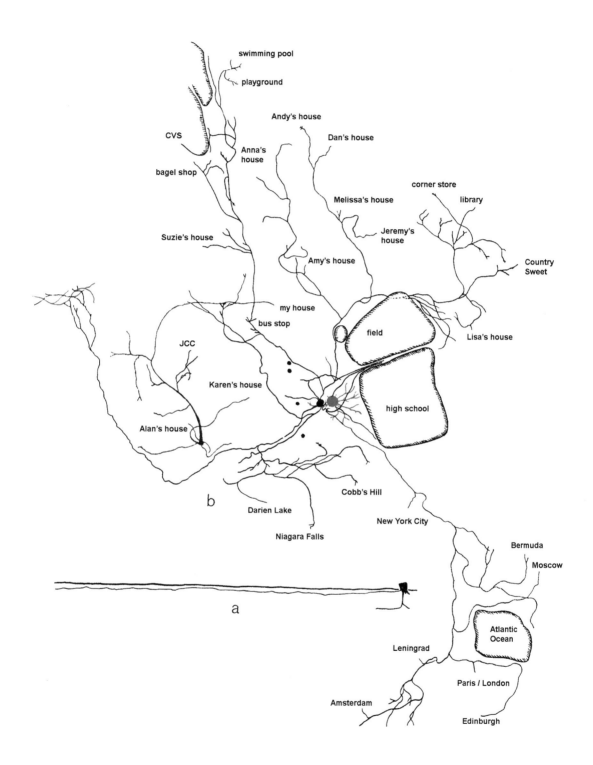

# PART 2

## HOW TO TELL
## IF YOU ARE HUMAN

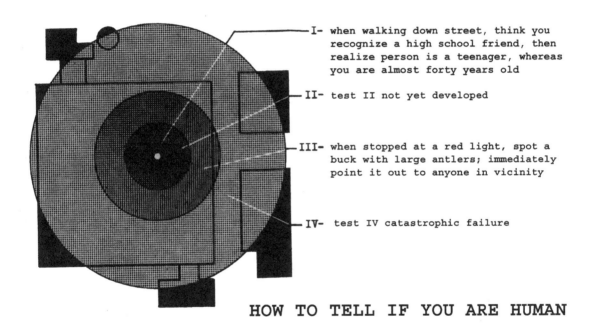

I- when walking down street, think you
recognize a high school friend, then
realize person is a teenager, whereas
you are almost forty years old

II- test II not yet developed

III- when stopped at a red light, spot a
buck with large antlers; immediately
point it out to anyone in vicinity

IV- test IV catastrophic failure

# HOW TO TELL IF YOU ARE HUMAN

My alcoholic father was banned from the public library in Buffalo, NY for playing the piano too loudly.

The library had an electric piano with headphones. My father used the headphones, but he banged the keys of the piano so forcefully that people complained.

This happened several times.

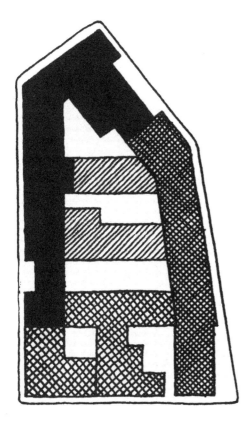

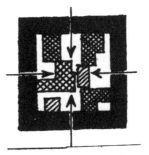

Wondering what the hell
trajectory I am on

# Baby Hygiene (Nursing) and Baby's Equipment

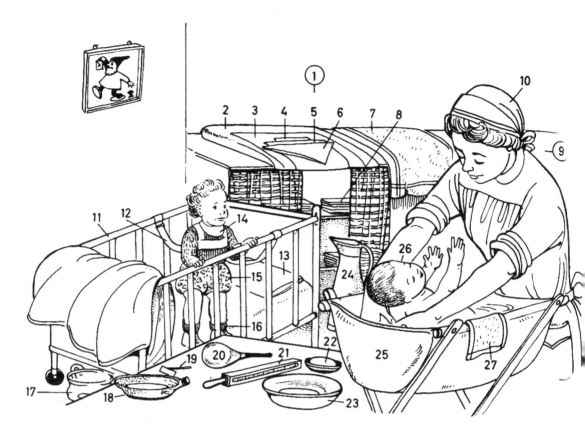

27
      your goal, of course

28

29 the tumbler (tumbling clown)

30 the mother (or a wet-nurse) feeding (nursing, wet-nursing) the baby (the nursing mother)

31
      is to get rid of all these things

32 the bassinet on wheels (basket crib on wheels):

33 the feather quilt

34 the lace flounce (lace frill)

35
      not as fast as possible

36

37 the nurse changing the baby (changing the baby's napkin)

38 the powder tin (dredging tin) with baby powder

39

40 the teething ring

41 the rubber animal

42 the baby's rattle (child's rattle)

43 the tin of ointment (tin of vaseline)

44
45
46
      but on a very particular
      schedule, with nothing
      happening too quickly
      or too slowly

47

48
      or it's all your fault

49

50

51 the dummy (comforter)

52

# The Children's Playground

**1-59 children's games** (games):

1 the game of

2

3

4 the game of

5
6
7
8
9
10
11
12
13 the game of
14

figuring out how
you are supposed
to be and how
you actually are
and who

15
16
17
18

who you are and how
to have fun and what
fun is

19
20

21
22
23 playing at                    the
game of
an active game
24 the game of
a game
25
26
27
28

29

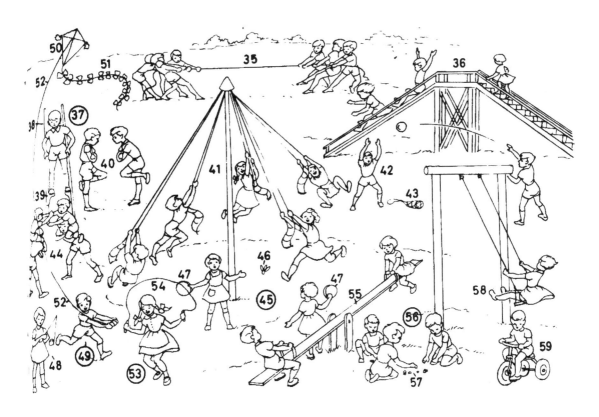

| | |
|---|---|
| 29 | and how to be safe |
| | and how much |
| 30 | to be safe and how |
| | little |
| | |
| 31 | |
| 32 | |
| 33 | |
| 34 | |
| 35 the game of | |
| 36 | |
| 37 | |
| 38 | |
| 39 | |
| | |
| 40 the        fight | |
| 41 | |
| 42 the game | |
| 43 | |

| | |
|---|---|
| 44 the        fight | |
| 45 the game | |
| | |
| 46 | |
| 47 | |
| 48 the game of | |
| 49 | |
| 50 | and how fast you can go |
| 51 | without hurting yourself |
| 52 | |
| 53 | |
| 54 | |
| | |
| 55 | |
| | |
| 56 the game of | |
| 57 | |
| 58 | |
| 59 | |

1
movies you
used to like

4
movies you
still like

7
movies you
never liked

2
movies you
haven't seen

5
movies you'll
never see

8
movies you've
forgotten

3
movies you
think you saw

6
movies that
don't exist

9
movies that
should exist

10

11

12

13

14
all the people you sat with at the movies

15

16

| 1300° | 1200° | 1100° | 1000° | 850° | 825° | 790° | 765° | 700° | 600° | 550° |
| --- | --- | --- | --- | --- | --- | --- | --- | --- | --- | --- |

I should probably
get going

please
ask me to stay

**period calculator**

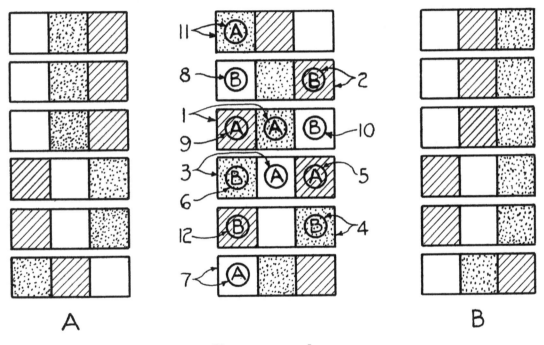

A

B

**disaster plan**

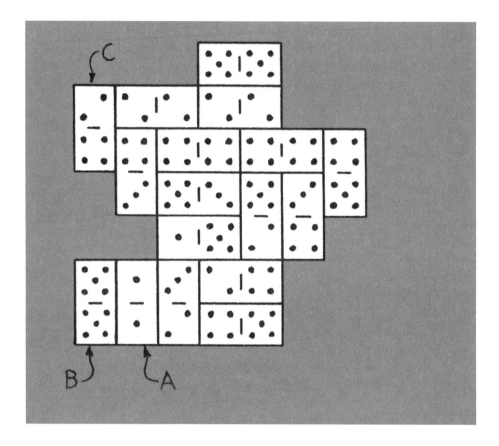

At the End of the Fifth Round

A. It's best to be first if you don't know what you're doing.
   They'll forgive your mistakes because you went first.

B. I don't like to be alone.

C. I wish I could get away from the endless counting and
   calculating. If I could just hold still for a moment, I know
   I'd feel all right.

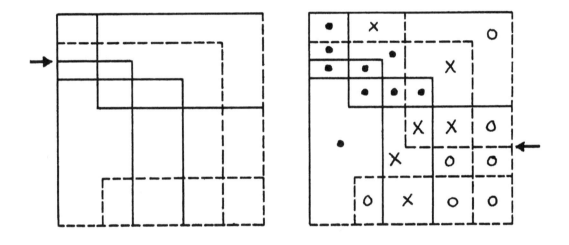

# I looked for you everywhere

chart showing that the way you listened to music when you were a teenager is similar but not identical to the way your children listen to music now

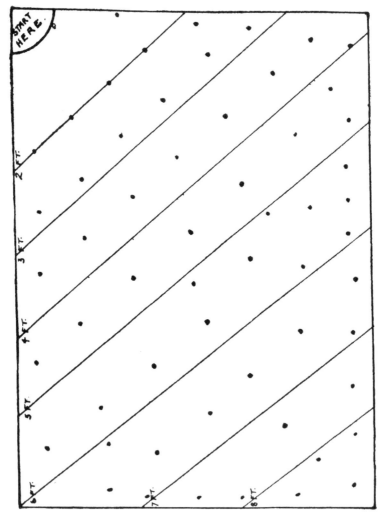

*One or two players*                    *Pencil and paper*

Teacher, I think there's something wrong with me

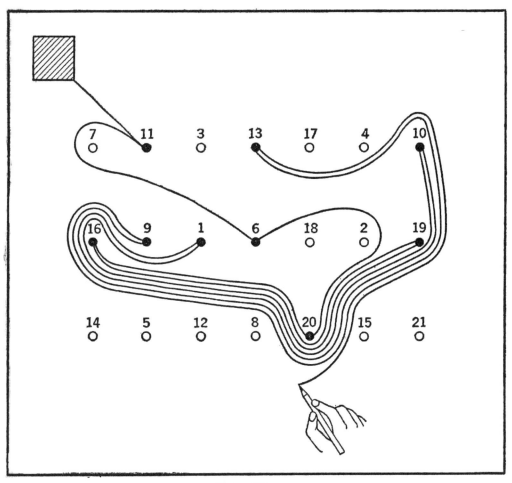

TAXI DRIVER

Sit on my lap sweetie

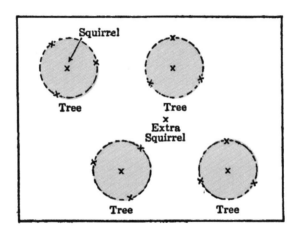

SQUIRRELS IN TREES

**Remarks.** Although there is really very little to this game it seems to appeal to little children very much and it is often asked for.

Players must figure out which is more important. It is impossible. Compare two squirrels and four trees. Squirrel and extra squirrel. Tree. Tree. Tree. Tree.

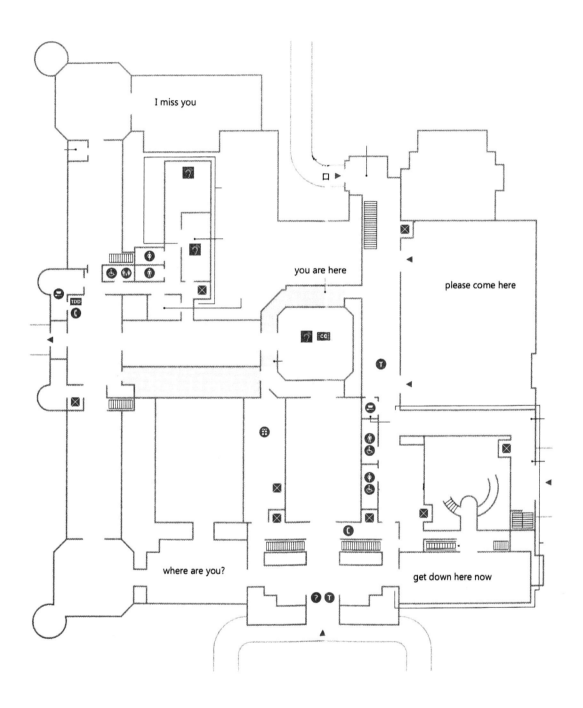

I miss you

you are here

please come here

where are you?

get down here now

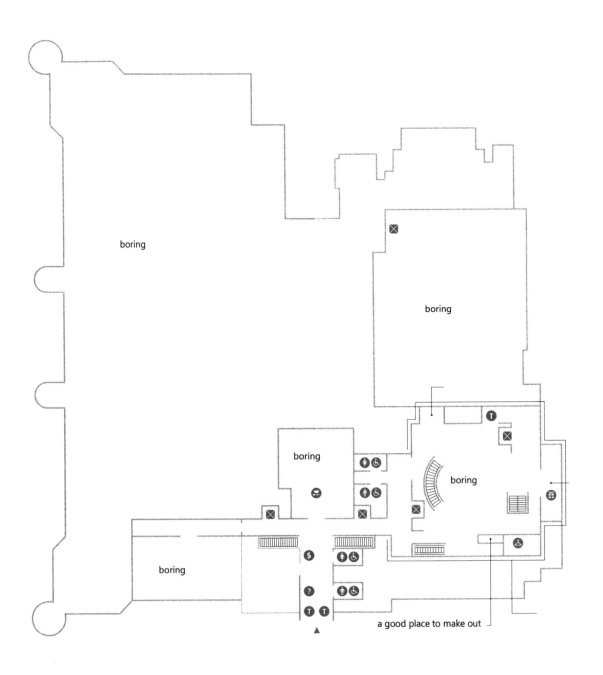

boring

boring

boring

boring

boring

boring

a good place to make out

how many times did each boyfriend say "I love you"?

not that I kept careful count

things you texted me

things you said to me in person

things you said as we fell asleep

things you whispered

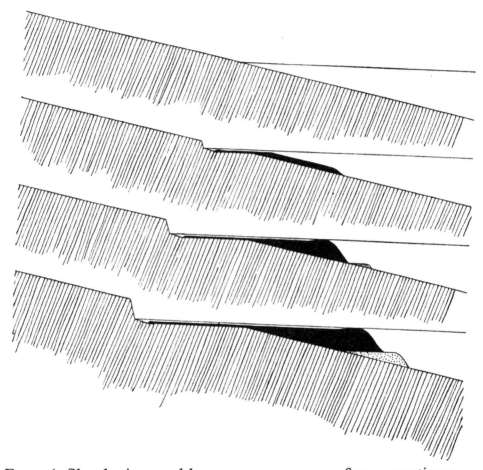

Fig. 36. Slowly, inexorably, over many years of conversations
and travels, they revealed their true natures. By the
time they knew all each other's flaws, it was too late
for them to stop being friends.

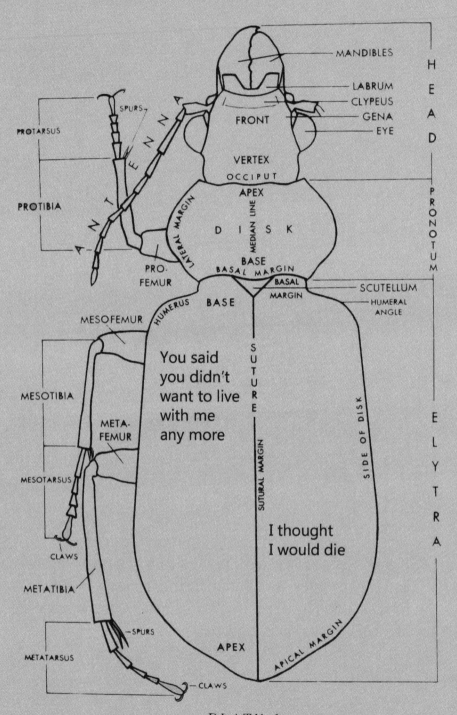

PLATE I

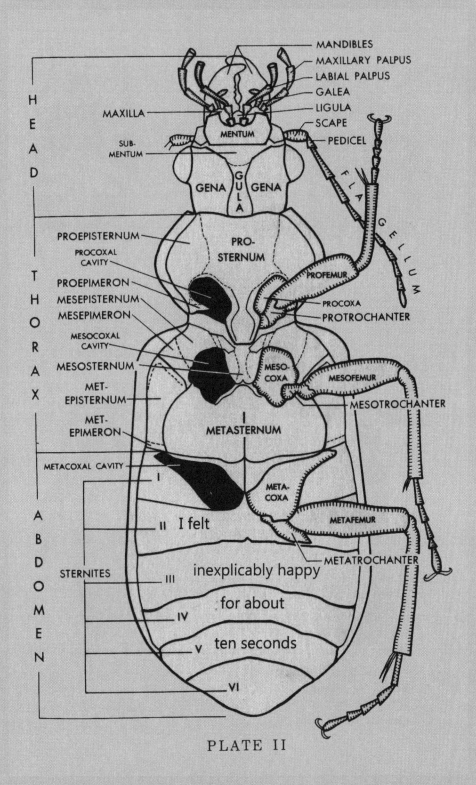

PLATE II

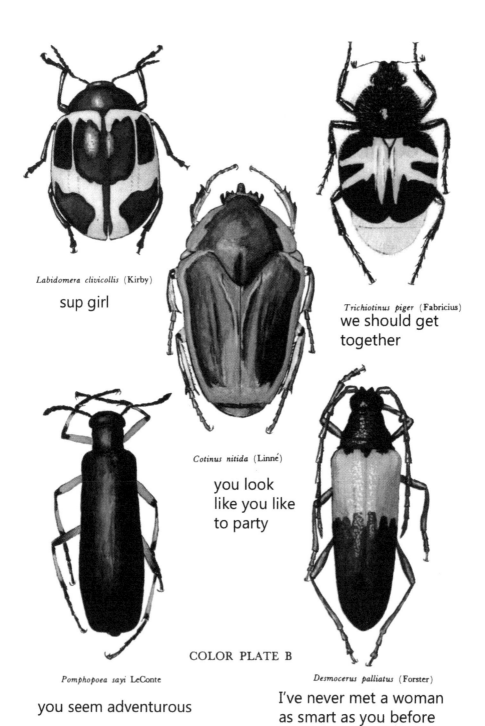

*Labidomera clivicollis* (Kirby)

sup girl

*Trichiotinus piger* (Fabricius)

we should get together

*Cotinus nitida* (Linné)

you look like you like to party

COLOR PLATE B

*Pomphopoea sayi* LeConte

you seem adventurous

*Desmocerus palliatus* (Forster)

I've never met a woman as smart as you before

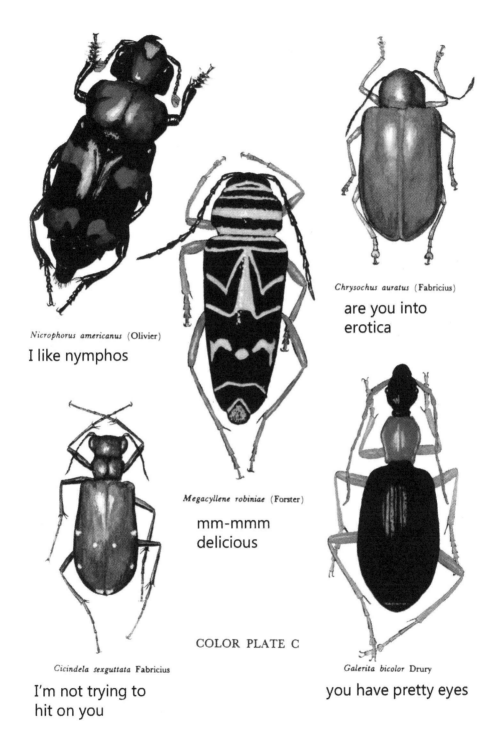

*Nicrophorus americanus* (Olivier)

I like nymphos

*Chrysochus auratus* (Fabricius)

are you into
erotica

*Megacyllene robiniae* (Forster)

mm-mmm
delicious

COLOR PLATE C

*Cicindela sexguttata* Fabricius

I'm not trying to
hit on you

*Galerita bicolor* Drury

you have pretty eyes

*Calosoma scrutator* Fabricius

COLOR PLATE A

You remind me of myself at your age

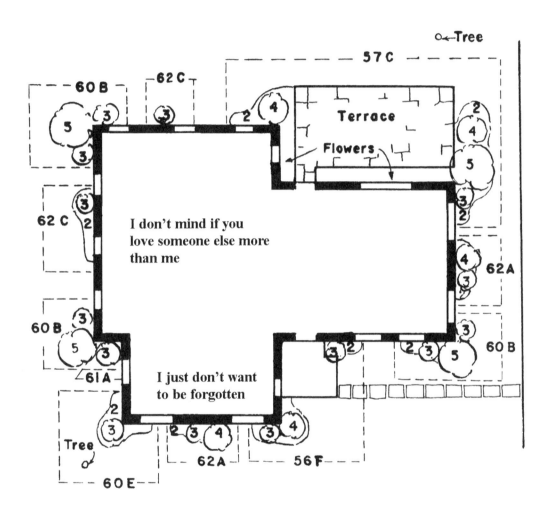

The diagram contains the following labels: Tree, 57 C, 60 B, 62 C, Terrace, Flowers, 62 C, 62 A, 60 B, 60 B, 61 A, Tree, 62 A, 56 F, 60 E

"I don't mind if you love someone else more than me"

"I just don't want to be forgotten"

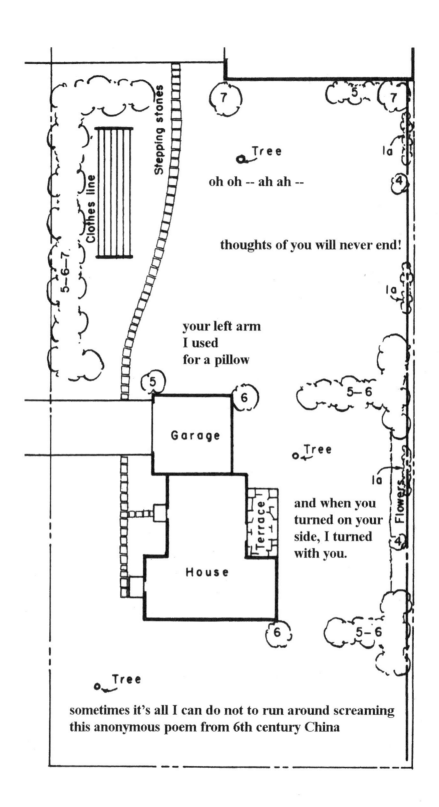

oh oh -- ah ah --

thoughts of you will never end!

your left arm
I used
for a pillow

and when you
turned on your
side, I turned
with you.

sometimes it's all I can do not to run around screaming
this anonymous poem from 6th century China

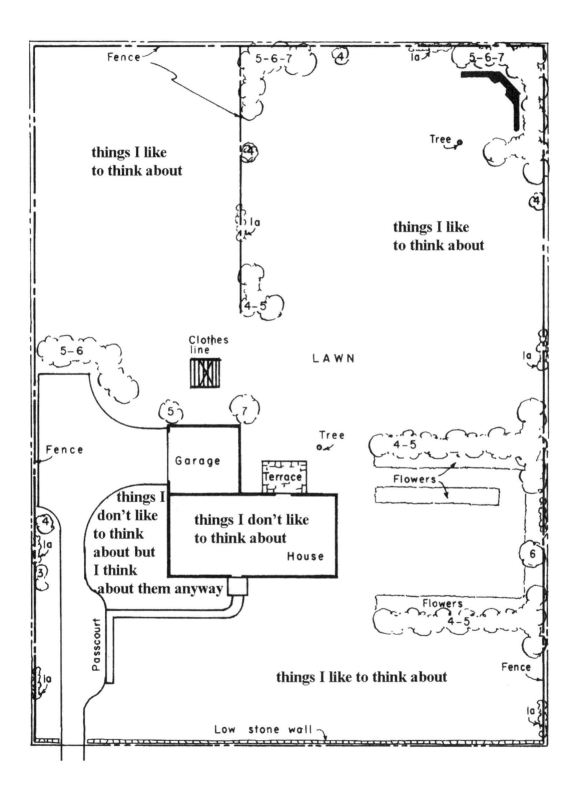

other people are all the same

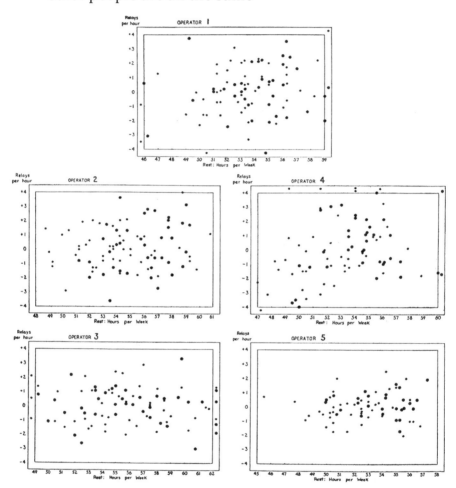

but not me, I'm different

## Diagram proving that you are my best friend

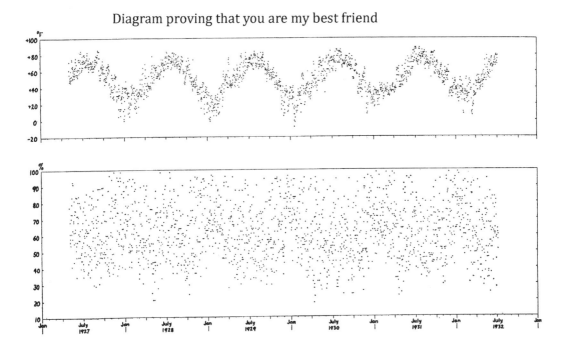

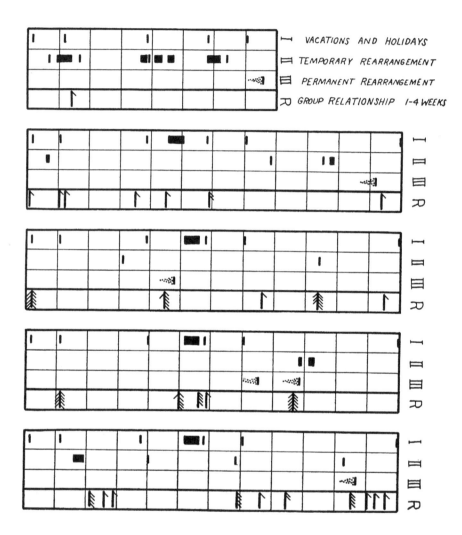

wedding seating chart showing which guests were involved with which other guests and when and how

# PART 3

# BE YOURSELF
# (BUT NOT TOO MUCH)

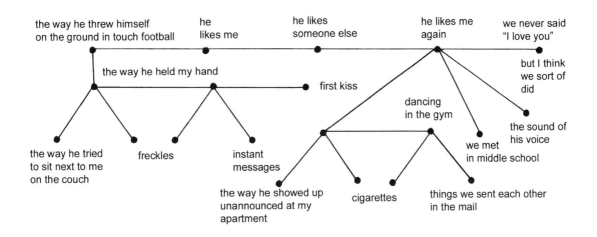

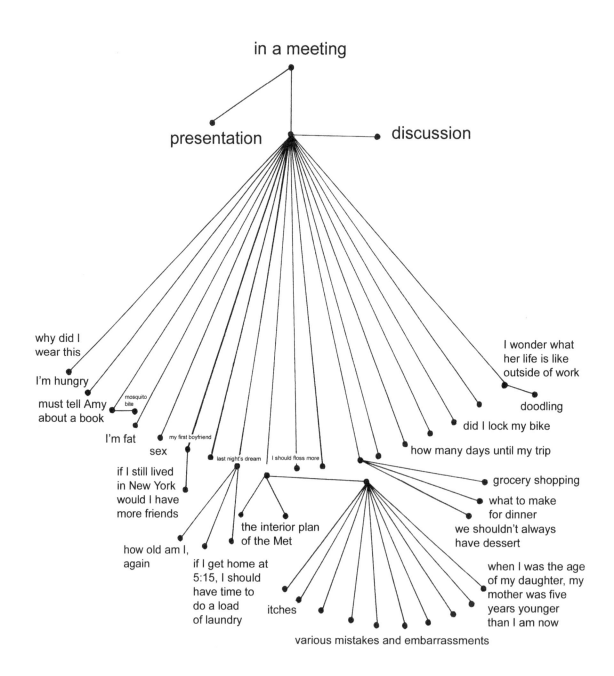

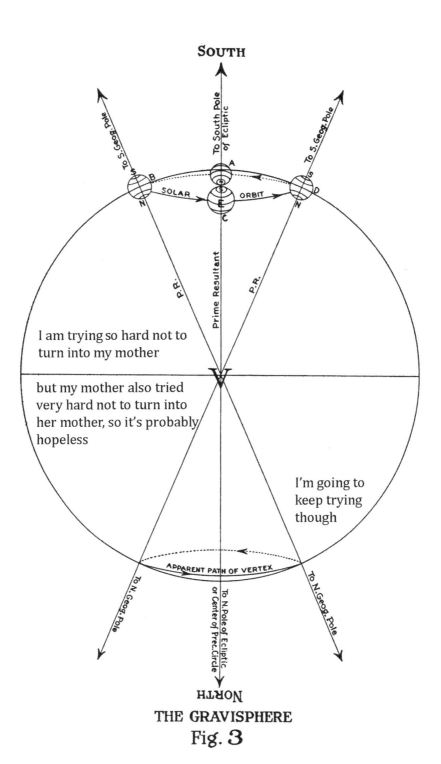

SOUTH

To South Pole of Ecliptic

To S. Geog. Pole

To S. Geog. Pole

SOLAR ORBIT

Prime Resultant

P.R.

P.R.

I am trying so hard not to turn into my mother

but my mother also tried very hard not to turn into her mother, so it's probably hopeless

I'm going to keep trying though

APPARENT PATH OF VERTEX

To N. Geog. Pole

To N.Pole of Ecliptic or Center of Prec. Circle

To N.Geog.Pole

NORTH

THE GRAVISPHERE
Fig. 3

while I make dinner
I think about eating dinner

TO VERNAL EQUINOX

while I eat dinner
I think about dessert

TO V.E.

while I watch TV
I think about reading

while I'm at work
I think about dinner

TO V.E.

when I wake up
I think about work

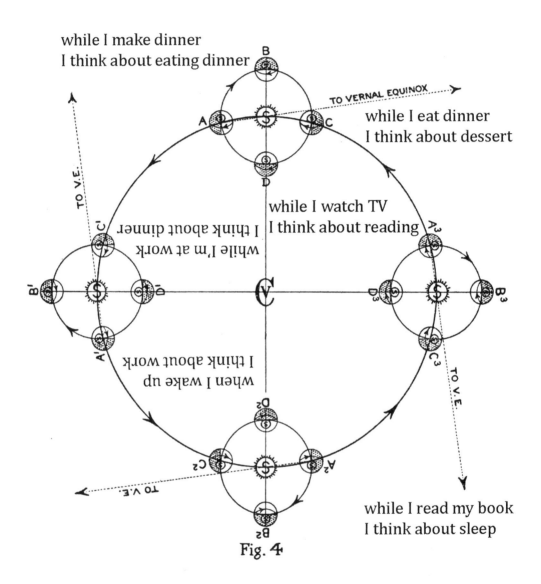

TO V.E.

while I read my book
I think about sleep

Fig. 4

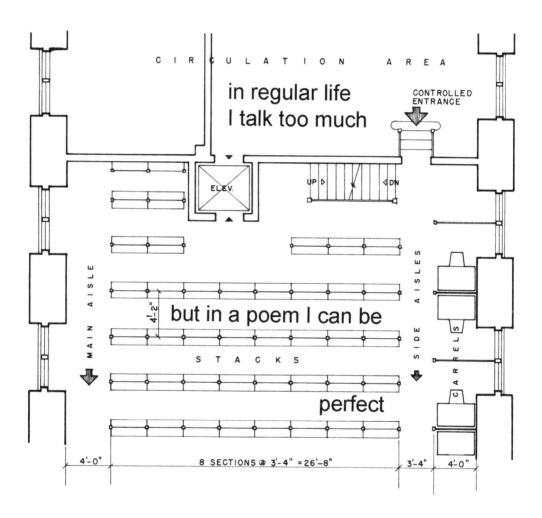

CIRCULATION AREA

in regular life
I talk too much

CONTROLLED
ENTRANCE

ELEV.

UP ▷          ◁ DN

MAIN AISLE

but in a poem I can be

4'-2"

SIDE AISLES

STACKS

CARRELS

perfect

4'-0"          8 SECTIONS @ 3'-4" = 26'-8"          3'-4"     4'-0"

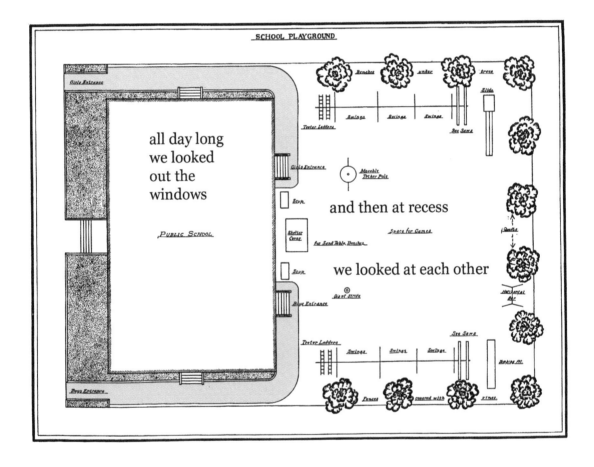

all day long
we looked
out the
windows

and then at recess

we looked at each other

we did exactly as we were told

even if we didn't understand why

we looked at each other
and knew we all felt the same

even though it didn't seem like
we were getting anywhere,
we kept going

# THE SIX SQUARE PUZZLE.

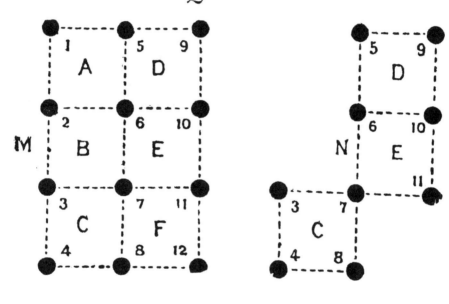

be yourself                    (but not too much)

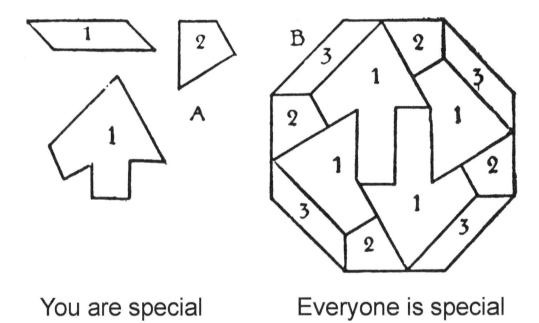

You are special          Everyone is special

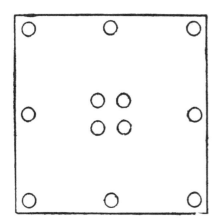

Please tell me what to do

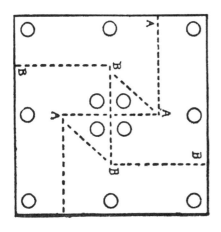

Stop telling me what to do

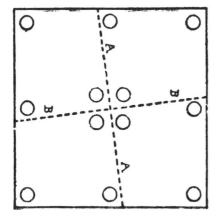

Please tell me what to do

In the grocery store, the check-out clerk tells me it's a good day to be alive. Is he in love? Did something wonderful happen to him? Or is it the opposite, is he talking himself out of a depression?

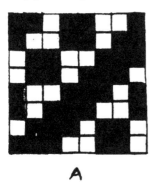

A

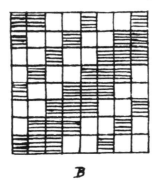

B

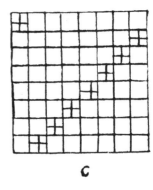

C

The woman in line behind me smiles and I smile back. We all agree, for a moment, that yes, it's a good day to be alive, and together, at Safeway at 2:45 p.m. on a Saturday in December,

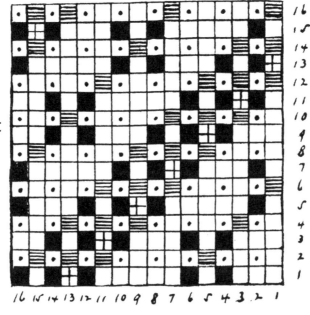

D

16 outside
15 temperature
14
13 48 degrees
12 Fahrenheit
11 in Colorado
10
9 Springs,
8 Colorado,
7 U.S.A., Earth,
6
5 the Solar
4 System, the
3 Milky Way
2
1 Galaxy, the
Universe.

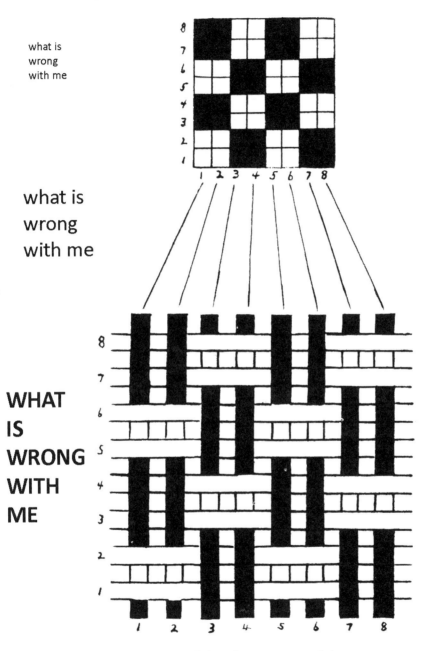

what is
wrong
with me

## what is
## wrong
## with me

**WHAT**
**IS**
**WRONG**
**WITH**
**ME**

something is wrong with me

When I saw you
I wanted to race
over and give you
a hug but I resisted
the impulse

I don't
know why

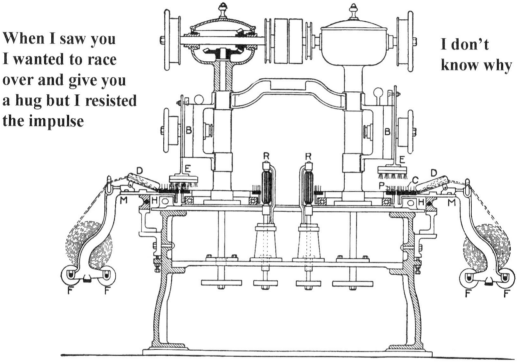

WOOLEN AND WORSTED — MANUFACTURE    139

Fig. 88. — Detail of Noble Comb.

From Collins' *Woolen and Worsted Spinning*, by courtesy of the American School of Correspondence.

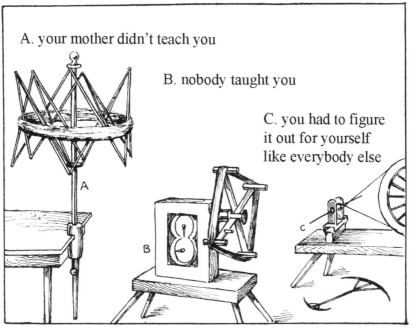

A. your mother didn't teach you

B. nobody taught you

C. you had to figure
it out for yourself
like everybody else

FIG. 8. — *A*, Swift; *B*, Clock Reel; *C*, Quill or Plug Winder; *D*, Niddy Noddy.

PLATE 52

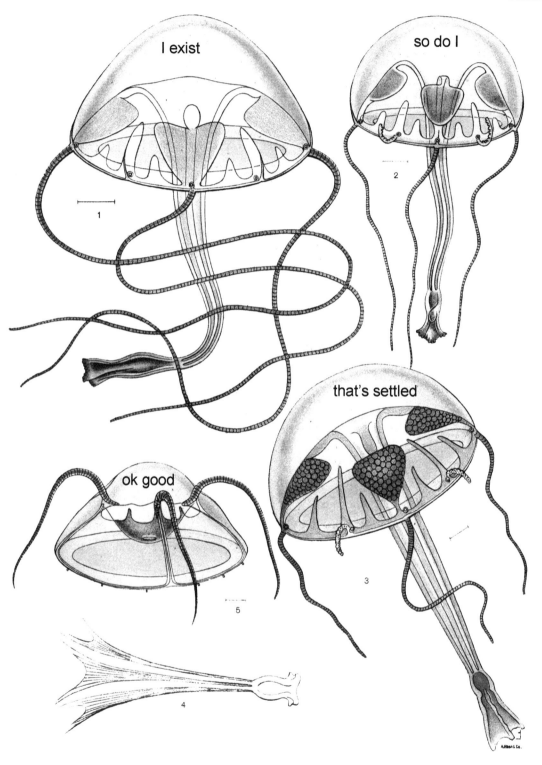